The Key to the Secret

MINA FARAWAY

ISBN 979-8-9851914-1-7

Acknowledgements

I deeply appreciate Napoleon Hill, Earl Nightingale, Rhonda Byrne, Jack Canfield, Bob Proctor, Eckhart Tolle, Mel Robbins, Oprah Winfrey, Abraham Hicks, and many others. Your authenticity, sincerity, and willingness to share your knowledge and wisdom led to the hidden gems in this book. I'm so happy and grateful to share them with those who are on their own journeys.

For news from Mina Faraway, visit
https://www.facebook.com/minafaraway

OR

Connect on social media at https://linktr.ee/minafaraway

~~~ **Coming Soon!** ~~~

The Key to the Secret Lock

Table of Contents

Introduction

"The subconscious mind is incalculably powerful, and can solve our problems if we go about it the right way. The best way is to hold in your mind, as often as possible, a clear picture of yourself already having accomplished your goal. You know what you want. Define it clearly and then project it clearly on the motion-picture screen of your mind. Hold it. See yourself doing the things and having the things you'll have when your objective will have been reached. Do this as often as possible as you go about your daily work, and especially at night, just before you go to sleep, and the first thing upon rising. As you do this, your subconscious will lead you in the most logical ways toward your objective. Don't fight it. Follow your sudden hunches, the ideas that come into your mind, knowing that it's your subconscious trying to get through to your conscious mind. If you'll keep at this, the wonderful ideas that just seem to come from nowhere will amaze and delight you."
~ Napoleon Hill, Think and Grow Rich

= =

This workbook is for you and about you. Its intention is to help you fulfill your purpose by guiding you step-by-step on your journey to manifesting the life of your dreams faster than you thought possible.

Chapter 1

Define Your Purpose

"Desire is the starting point of all achievement, not a hope, not a wish, but a keen pulsating desire which transcends everything. When your desires are strong enough, you will appear to possess superhuman
powers to achieve."
~ Napoleon Hill

= =

Real-Life Story:

Jeb's* university campus police department opened 3 internship positions to work in the department. The list of requirements included a Criminal Justice major. Jeb felt law enforcement was his purpose in life, but he had no law enforcement experience and was not majoring in Criminal Justice. Instead of worrying about not being chosen, every day he visualized himself as a police officer, helping people and catching criminals, and took steps to learn everything he could about being a police officer. Over 210 students applied for the internships, but the police department hired Jeb. When the police academy opened only a few positions for state-certified police training, they hired Jeb. He has been a police officer for 28 years.

*Names have been changed to protect privacy.

= =

This is the biggest step of all on your Law of Attraction journey. You must know what you want, what your passion is, what your purpose is in order to have a journey to begin. You must know what you want to do or be in life. Even if you think you don't know, you may simply be resisting it. Explore your interests. Is there anything in your life you would do, even if you weren't being paid to do it? Don't worry about whether you think you can make a living from it or not yet. If you don't have a goal, you can't achieve it.

Deep down inside, you know what your passion is, your calling, your purpose in life. It's whatever you're excited about when you wake up every morning, no matter how silly or superficial it seems. It gives you energy. It fills you with joy. You lose track of time when you're doing it. Dream big. You are important. Your dreams are important. Your life's purpose is important.

Now describe your passion in detail. Feel the love, the excitement, and the joy it brings you. Hold on to those feelings as you take time to jot down any words, sentences, ideas, or drawings that describe what you think and how you feel about your purpose:

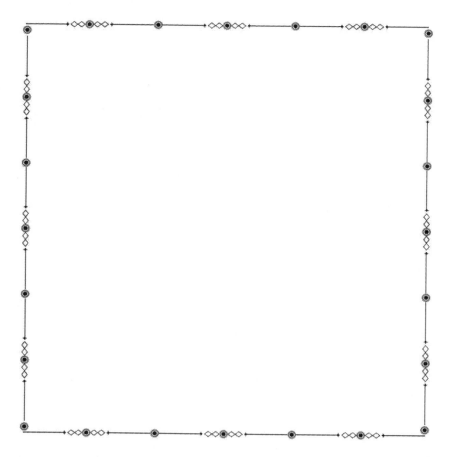

After you're done brainstorming, write it down in a statement that announces your purpose to yourself and to the world:

My Purpose:

_____

_____

_____

_____

_____

_____

Chapter 2

What You Will Provide in Exchange for Success

"Not everybody can be famous, but everybody can be great because greatness is
determined by service. You only need a heart full of grace
and a soul generated by love."
~ Martin Luther King Jr.

= =

Real-Life Story:

Ren's passion is the creative aspect of designing websites, and he knows there is
demand for his services. He watches all the videos he can find on developing his
skills and signs up for notifications on new videos. He listens to podcasts on
developing websites and joins several Facebook groups where he can interact
with others in the same field. He also created a profile on a freelancing site for
minor projects to gain experience. Every spare moment he has, he researches,
studies, and talks to others on the latest and greatest techniques and tools. Every
day, he increases his experience and proficiency.*

= =

Before you can receive money for delivering on the services, goods or
profession related to your life's purpose, you may need specialized knowledge
or training. Set aside time in your day to learn all you can about your chosen
subject. Work hard to gain the skills, knowledge, and expertise needed to earn
your fortune. Find others who do what you do and spend most of your time
with them.

If you don't have the resources to pay for training courses or higher-level
education, you can train and educate yourself with whatever free resources
you can find. Even if there are no mentoring groups near you, the people you
watch, listen to, or interact with online are your mentors as well. The

information is out there; spend your time and energy on it to make your dreams a reality.

Note: You don't need to know *how* you will succeed; you just take one step at a time to put yourself on the right path to find success. Writing down the next step you need to take, one step at a time, may help you define a plan on how to get there faster. Estimate the time you will spend honing your skills, or training, educating, and motivating yourself each day to reach your goal:

Step: **Daily Time:**

_____   _____

Step: **Daily Time:**

_____   _____

Step: **Daily Time:**

_____   _____

Step: **Daily Time:**

_____   _____

Step: **Daily Time:**

_____   _____

Step: **Daily Time:**

_____   _____

Chapter 3

When You Will Achieve Your Purpose

"You are the master of your destiny. You can influence, direct, and control your own environment. You can make your life what you want it to be."
~ Napoleon Hill

= =

Real-Life Story:

Eva* visualizes herself selling a million dollar home each month as a real estate agent. She immerses herself in the happiness and appreciation she feels in achieving her goal and recites the following every day before going to sleep and first thing in the morning:

By December, 31st, 20__ at 23:59, I have $30,000 a month in income, which comes to me in varying amounts from time to time between now and then.

In return for this money, I give the most efficient real estate guidance and advice of which I'm capable, rendering the fullest possible quantity and the best possible quality of real estate service in my capacity.**

**Adapted from Think and Grow Rich, by Napoleon Hill

= =

Fill in the affirmation below with your life's purpose. Include the service, product, or profession you will exchange for wealth and abundance. Be specific on the date and time you will achieve this. Read it out loud every morning and every evening or several times a day. Hang the statement up in several prominent places to remind you of your goal:

By _____at _____, I have _____ a month in income, which comes to me in varying amounts from time to time between now and then.

In return for this money, I give the most efficient_____ of which I'm capable, rendering the fullest possible quantity and the best possible quality of_____ in my capacity.

By _____at _____, I have _____ a month in income, which comes to me in varying amounts from time to time between now and then.

In return for this money, I give the most efficient_____ of which I'm capable, rendering the fullest possible quantity and the best possible quality of_____ in my capacity.

By _____at _____, I have _____ a month in income, which comes to me in varying amounts from time to time between now and then.

In return for this money, I give the most efficient_____ of which I'm capable, rendering the fullest possible quantity and the best possible quality of_____ in my capacity.

Chapter 4

Have Faith and Confidence

"Ask, and it shall be given you; seek, and ye shall find; knock, and it shall be opened unto you: for every one that asketh receiveth; and he that seeketh findeth; and to him that knocketh it shall be opened."
~ Matthew 7:7-8 KJV

= =

Real-Life Story:

As an artist, Amanda* recites the following to herself every night and every morning to reprogram her mind into believing she can achieve her purpose, her goals, and her desires:

I have this money in my possession now. My faith is so strong that I see this money before my eyes, and I can touch it with my hands. It transfers to me at the time and in the proportion that I deliver the artistic work I render for it. I have a plan by which to accumulate this money and I'm following that plan to receive it.**

**Adapted from Think and Grow Rich, by Napoleon Hill

= =

Visualization, belief, and taking action are fundamental to achieving your purpose. Fill in the blank with your service, product, or profession and recite the affirmation at least twice a day, every day, to instill in you the belief and confidence that you already have exactly what you want. Attach the statement to your goal statement in the same places where you will see both throughout the day. As you read them, feel the energy and joy of the affirmation:

I have this money in my possession now; my faith is so strong that I see this money before my eyes, and I can touch it with my hands. It transfers to me at the time and in the proportion that I deliver _____ I render for it. I have a plan by which to accumulate this money and I am following that plan to receive it.

I have this money in my possession now; my faith is so strong that I see this money before my eyes, and I can touch it with my hands. It transfers to me at the time and in the proportion that I deliver _____ I render for it. I have a plan by which to accumulate this money and I am following that plan to receive it.

I have this money in my possession now; my faith is so strong that I see this money before my eyes, and I can touch it with my hands. It transfers to me at the time and in the proportion that I deliver _____ I render for it. I have a plan by which to accumulate this money and I am following that plan to receive it.

I have this money in my possession now; my faith is so strong that I see this money before my eyes, and I can touch it with my hands. It transfers to me at the time and in the proportion that I deliver _____ I render for it. I have a plan by which to accumulate this money and I am following that plan to receive it.

I have this money in my possession now; my faith is so strong that I see this money before my eyes, and I can touch it with my hands. It transfers to me at the time and in the proportion that I deliver _____ I render for it. I have a plan by which to accumulate this money and I am following that plan to receive it.

Chapter 5

Embrace Your Negative Thoughts

"Your life is in your hands. No matter where you are now, no matter what has happened in your life, you can begin to consciously choose your thoughts, and you can change your life. If you're feeling good, then you're creating a future that's on track with your desires. If you're feeling bad, you're creating a future that's off track with your desires."
~ Rhonda Byrne

= =

Real-Life Story:

Sajan* lost his job suddenly and without notice, making him feel insecure, fearful, and despairing. His job hadn't given him joy and didn't relate to his life's purpose, but it had paid the bills. He knew what he wanted to do, what gave him joy and purpose, but he feared he wouldn't succeed and that his family and friends would criticize him. Realizing those negative feelings were holding him back from taking action, he opened his arms wide and visualized hugging all his negative thoughts. It surprised him how quickly those feelings dissipated and how much better he felt. Then, he thought about the things that made him happy and celebrated how grateful those positive thoughts made him. Whenever he felt doubt or fear, he practiced welcoming his negative thoughts and feelings.**

**Adapted from The Greatest Secret by Rhonda Byrne

= =

Your thoughts become things. If you spend your time focusing on negative things, that's what you'll receive. However, it's okay to have negative thoughts; don't fight them, but don't dwell on them, either. Negative thoughts and feelings are not you. You can dissolve those thoughts and feelings faster by embracing them, rather than fighting them.

When you have negative thoughts, write them down here. Then embrace them mentally and emotionally, wait for them to dissipate, and then cross them off your list. Do this as many times as needed to take the power away from the negativity and move your energy to the positive thoughts, ideas, and feelings that make you abundantly happy. It will happen faster and easier each time.

Replace the negative with a positive affirmation. You may think, "Others are better at _____ than me." Replace this negative thought with the affirmation, "I am excellent at _____." Cross off your negative thoughts and focus on the positive affirmations!

Negative Thought or Feeling: **Positive Affirmation:**

_____   _____

_____   _____

_____   _____

_____   _____

_____   _____

_____   _____

_____   _____

_____   _____

Chapter 6

Live Your Ideal Schedule

"Create a definite plan for carrying out your desire and begin at once,
whether you are ready or not, to put this plan into action."
~ Napoleon Hill

= =

Real-Life Story:

Chad* wanted to be a successful business consultant, helping businesses grow their online sales, but with a full-time job in a different field, and a family to support, he couldn't quit his current job to do what he loved. Instead, he created his ideal schedule as if he were a self-employed consultant, from the moment he woke to the moment he slept. He included mealtimes, exercise, career training and all the activities he would do as a business consultant. Then, he added 1 hour for training during his lunchtime. He added another hour in the evening after work. He lived his schedule and replaced whatever time he could during the day with activities, thoughts, and feelings related to building a consulting business. When he couldn't actually do these activities, he visualized himself doing them. One day, he realized he had gradually replaced his employment income with business consulting income. He couldn't believe how fast it had happened once he'd set his mind to it. Chad is now a self-employed consultant with a flexible work schedule and complete control over his income. He loves what he does, and he's good at it. He makes more money now than he ever thought possible.

= =

When you follow your purpose, then people, events, and opportunities all align to make it happen. Write out your ideal schedule as if you are doing what you love, so you visualize exactly how your day will go. Find times and ways to do whatever activities you can that actively pursue your purpose. Set calendar or phone alerts to help you stay on track. Looking back, it will surprise you at how quickly your ideal schedule became your reality.

Note: See the next chapter *Fool Yourself into Your Passion* for additional tips on visualizing actively pursuing your passion through living your schedule.

Fill out your schedule and hang it in several places to make it easier to follow and visualize each activity throughout the day:

Time   **Activity**

————   ———————————————————————

————   ———————————————————————

————   ———————————————————————

————   ———————————————————————

————   ———————————————————————

————   ———————————————————————

————   ———————————————————————

————   ———————————————————————

————   ———————————————————————

————   ———————————————————————

————   ———————————————————————

Time	Activity
——	————————————
——	————————————
——	————————————
——	————————————
——	————————————
——	————————————
——	————————————
——	————————————
——	————————————
——	————————————
——	————————————
——	————————————
——	————————————
——	————————————
——	————————————
——	————————————

Time	Activity
————	————————————————
————	————————————————
————	————————————————
————	————————————————
————	————————————————
————	————————————————
————	————————————————
————	————————————————
————	————————————————
————	————————————————
————	————————————————
————	————————————————
————	————————————————
————	————————————————
————	————————————————
————	————————————————

Chapter 7

Fool Yourself into Your Passion

"Whatever goal you give to your subconscious mind, it will work night and day to achieve."~ Jack Canfield

= =

Real-Life Story:

Lateesha* created her schedule as if she were a best-selling author. Even when she worked her day job as a project manager, she visualized she was writing, not working. When she talked to a client, she pretended to be talking to a publisher who was offering a large book advance to publish her books. The more imaginative she was, the more she enjoyed the game because it made her happy. The happier she felt, and the more she pretended to be living the life she wanted, the more people, places, and events aligned to make it happen. At the end of the day, she felt she had spent her time writing, not working. Within 30 days, her life had completely changed. She had published her first book and finished 2 author interviews when she realized, "Wow, that didn't take long at all!"

= =

"Fake it till you make it" is a phrase that means if you pretend to have confidence and competence, you will feel more confident and competent. This is the same as visualizing, believing, and having faith that you have what you want already. Visualize the outcome as you're living the activities that lead to that outcome by imagining it. Pretend, through your thoughts and feelings, you are doing the activities you love. Revel in the excitement.

Think about the things you do now that are not along the lines of your purpose in life and come up with a substitute action or thought about your passion you can imagine doing instead that brings you joy and fulfills you.

Then get ready, because faking it until you make it will happen faster than you expect!

When I'm: I'm actually:

_____   _____

_____   _____

_____   _____

_____   _____

_____   _____

_____   _____

_____   _____

_____   _____

_____   _____

_____   _____

_____   _____

_____   _____

_____   _____

_____   _____

Chapter 8

Visualize Your Day

"You only have control over three things in your life. The thoughts you think, the images you visualize, and the actions you take."
~ Jack Canfield

= =

Real-Life Story:

David* loved waking up at 5:30 am. First, he meditated, then exercised before breakfast. Then, he worked for 3 hours, ate a snack and spent 15 minutes organizing his desk and office. Having a clean workspace allowed him to be calmer and more efficient at work. He spent lunch laughing and joking with his favorite coworkers. He worked several more hours and made more money than he thought possible. He exercised, then headed home for dinner, and to spend time with his family. Before bed, he wrote in his gratitude journal, read his affirmations, and visualized his tomorrow.

= =

Visualize the next day before you go to sleep at night and when you wake up the next day. This solidifies the schedule you've created filled with activities that fulfill your passion and purpose. It will help you stay on-track and thinking, feeling, and manifesting your desires. Your days will be full of joy and be more fulfilling as the Universe moves people, resources, and opportunities to help you fulfill your purpose:

Tomorrow will be:

Tomorrow will be:

_____

Tomorrow will be:

_____

Tomorrow will be:

_____

Tomorrow will be:

_____

Tomorrow will be:

_____

Tomorrow will be:

_____

Tomorrow will be:

_____

Tomorrow will be:

_____

Tomorrow will be:

_____

Chapter 9

Gratitude Practices

"The heart that gives thanks is a happy one, for we cannot feel thankful
and unhappy at the same time."
~ Douglas Wood

= =

Real-Life Story:

Before sleep, Milena reviewed her day and wrote about her appreciation for
everything she saw, felt, thought, and experienced throughout the day. She
appreciated most of all the moments when she was happiest, peaceful, or
content. After each entry, she said aloud, "Thank you, thank you, thank you."*

= =

Begin every day and every night with the following gratitude practice to revel
in feelings of happiness and appreciation for what you have. Include
everything currently on your list of desires!

I'm so happy and grateful for...

_____

_____

_____

_____

I'm so happy and grateful for...

_____

_____

_____

I'm so happy and grateful for...

_____

_____

_____

_____

I'm so happy and grateful for...

_____

_____

_____

_____

I'm so happy and grateful for...

_____

_____

_____

_____

I'm so happy and grateful for...

_____

_____

_____

_____

I'm so happy and grateful for...

_____

_____

_____

_____

Chapter 10

Let Go - You Have it Already!

"Let go of doubts and start believing that you can do whatever
it is you set out to do." ~ Jack Canfield

= =

Real-Life Story:

Esmée practiced the Law of Attraction but struggled with how to "let it go."
She was emotionally invested in what she wanted, so she didn't understand how
she could stop wanting something enough to get it. That's when she realized the
emotions of "wanting" and "needing" were focused on the feeling of lack.
When she started using her vivid imagination and all 5 of her senses to pretend
she had the things she wanted already, that feeling of scarcity disappeared.
Some days were easier than others, but she made it into a game every day.*

= =

Believe you have it already. This is the hardest part of the Law of Attraction,
but with all the previous steps put together and living your daily schedule as
if you have already achieved your purpose, you will have accomplished the
hardest part of the manifestation process!

Practice letting go of the *needing, wanting,* or *lacking* feelings. Those feelings
draw you back into the reality of not having what you want. Stay focused on
having and the joy it brings you. Be aware of your state of mind, stay positive,
and embrace any negative thoughts. Keep to your schedule as closely as
possible to stay focused on convincing yourself you have everything you desire
now.

List the things you have trouble letting go here. Then, cross them off to symbolize you have received it and have let the desire for it go:

I'm so happy and grateful I wanted and then received:

_____

_____

_____

_____

_____

_____

_____

_____

_____

_____

_____

_____

_____

Chapter 11

Act on Inspired Ideas

"Luck is preparation meeting the moment of opportunity. There is no luck without
you being prepared to handle that moment of opportunity."
~ Oprah Winfrey

= =

Real-Life Story:

Eva wanted to be a romance novelist. While she was writing her first novel,
she set up a website and social media accounts under her pseudonym. One day,
another name came to her out of nowhere. Even though it meant spending more
money and effort to set up a new website and the social media accounts under
the new name, she acted on her inspired idea. Only then did she realize the
meaning of the new pseudonym meant "love" and "dreamy". Taking action
and listening to her inspired thoughts led her to the perfect pen name for a
romance novelist living her true purpose.*

= =

When you are living your passion and purpose, the Universe will provide the
people, resources, and opportunities to make your dreams happen. Make sure
you act on those to keep the process going!

Write down the inspired thoughts, ideas and feelings that come to you, then
act on them:

Inspired Idea: _____

Inspired Idea: _____

Inspired Idea: _____

Inspired Idea: _____

Inspired Idea: _____

Inspired Idea: _____

Inspired Idea: _____

Inspired Idea: _____

Inspired Idea: _____

Inspired Idea: _____

Inspired Idea: _____

Inspired Idea: _____

Inspired Idea: _____

Inspired Idea: _____

Inspired Idea: _____

Inspired Idea: _____

Inspired Idea: _____

Inspired Idea: _____

Inspired Idea: _____

Inspired Idea: _____

Inspired Idea: _____

Inspired Idea: _____

amazon.com

SQvYLKJVtG

Order of August 24, 2024

Qty.	Item
1	**The Key to the Secret: 15 Fast and Easy Steps to Achieving What You Want Now** Faraway, Mina --- Paperback **B09KF4GLM8** B09KF4GLM8 9798985191417

Return or replace your item
Visit Amazon.com/returns

0/QvYLKJVtG/-1 of 1-//MOB5-TWI/std-n-us/0/0825-23:30/0825-06:35

C4-
M2

Chapter 12

"Donate" Your Bills and Debt

"Money comes easily and frequently."
~ Loral Langemeier

= =

Real-Life Story:

When it's time to pay his bills, Anwil* appreciates having access to the goods and services he needs to run his business and support his family. As he writes the checks or transfers the amounts for these bills, he says thank you for having the money to pay them. He visualizes the money going out and coming back to him in larger sums. The more money he sends out, the more that comes in. He appreciates being able to keep it circulating.

Method #1:

When you pay your bills, visualize the money circulating to and from you. Know that the money you pay for the goods and services you need is also supporting the people, things, and businesses you use. Your job is to keep it circulating, so it goes out and comes back in larger amounts.

Real-Life Story:

When Petra* pays her bills, she visualizes having plenty of money to spare. It makes her happy to write her checks or transfer her money to the charities of her choice.

Method #2:

As you pay your bills, pretend you're donating the money to the charities and organizations that mean the most to you and make you happy. Include any tithing or businesses you want to support that help solve local or world problems. Revel in how much you enjoy helping make the world a better place.

= =

Choose whichever method for paying your bills and paying off debt resonates most with you and makes you happiest. Recite the affirmations below as you pay your bills:

I am so happy and grateful to be able to pay my bills and to send the money away, knowing it will come back to me in greater amounts.

I am so happy and grateful to donate and contribute money to my favorite people, charities, organizations, and businesses that make a difference in the world.

My Bill: **My Donation:**

_____   _____

_____   _____

_____   _____

_____   _____

_____   _____

_____   _____

_____   _____

Chapter 13

Place Your Order with the Universe

"Decide what you want. Believe you can have it. Believe that you deserve it and believe it's possible for you." ~ Jack Canfield

= =

Real-Life Story:

As a single mom, Brisa* had a tight budget. Her shallow kitchen sink made it difficult to prepare a turkey for her family's holiday dinner. Every day, she visualized preparing a turkey in a deeper sink. She asked the Universe for a new sink, let the joy of how that would feel wash over her, and then let it go. She was just happy to have food to feed her family for the holidays. A few days later, she talked to a neighbor, who remodeled kitchens. He mentioned his client had a deep, unwanted sink. Her neighbor offered to install the sink for free. Brisa appreciated the neighbor's client, her neighbor, and the universe for a new deep sink in which to prepare her family's dinner. Every time she used the sink, she said with all her heart, "Thank you!"

= =

The "I have" column is for your desires. The "It makes me feel" column is for visualizing yourself accepting it, receiving it, and even unwrapping it to help you feel the joy and excitement you will feel in that moment.

You can be as specific as you want in the details and above all, have fun! *Note:* Cross your desires off when you receive them, so you see your progress.

Place your order with the Universe!

I have: _____ It makes me feel: _____

I have: _____ It makes me feel: _____

I have: _____ It makes me feel: _____

I have: _____ It makes me feel: _____

I have: _____ It makes me feel: _____

I have: _____ It makes me feel: _____

I have: _____ It makes me feel: _____

I have: _____ It makes me feel: _____

I have: _____ It makes me feel: _____

I have: _____ It makes me feel: _____

I have: _____ It makes me feel: _____

I have: _____ It makes me feel: _____

I have: _____ It makes me feel: _____

I have: _____ It makes me feel: _____

I have: _____ It makes me feel: _____

I have: _____ It makes me feel: _____

I have: _____ It makes me feel: _____

I have: _____ It makes me feel: _____

I have: _____ It makes me feel: _____

I have: _____ It makes me feel: _____

Chapter 14

Describe Your Ideal Relationships

"You demonstrate love by giving it unconditionally to yourself. And as you do, you
attract others into your life who are able to love you,
without conditions."
~ Paul Ferrini

= =

Real-Life Story:

Lubov wanted a boyfriend. She had only 3 requirements; he would be tall,
muscular, and love her. She visualized him every day. A few months later, she
met him. Their relationship lasted only two years because they had very
different life goals, and she learned to be more specific. The next time, she listed
52 positive characteristics she wanted in a husband. She read the list every few
days and visualized their life together. She made room in her closet for his
clothes and cleared a drawer in the bathroom for his personal items. 2 years
later, she met a man with every single characteristic on her list, except for one.
Her list stated he would be bilingual, which he wasn't. However, he was a
citizen of 3 different countries. She laughingly said it still counted and
married him anyway.*

= =

Make a list of the characteristics you desire most in your relationships,
whether they apply to a romantic partner, a business partner, or your friends
and family. The intent is to attract the important people in your life with the
characteristics you value most, or if you are currently in those relationships,
to reinforce those attributes. Use positive terms. For example, write "active"
or "honest" instead of "not lazy" and "doesn't lie." Feel how happy you are to
be surrounded by people with the values and characteristics you treasure
most. The more specific you are, the better.

Characteristics I appreciate in my relationships:

_____

_____

_____

_____

_____

_____

_____

_____

_____

_____

_____

_____

_____

_____

_____

Chapter 15

A Contract with the Universe

"Set a goal to achieve something that is so big, so exhilarating that it
excites you and scares you at the same time."
~ Bob Proctor

= =

Real-Life Story:

Leif loved his job. He woke up every day, ready to do what he enjoyed and what
he was good at. He read his affirmations every morning and every night,
confident that he exchanged his service for a happy and abundant life. He lived
each day thinking, learning, and doing the activities that helped him achieve
his purpose. He said no to anything not aligned with his goals. He appreciated
the guidance, help, ideas and opportunities he received and the confirmation
he was on the right path. He paid his bills by "donating" to those who helped
him along the way and gave him what he needed, when he needed it. He was
happy and grateful to donate to the charities, organizations and causes that
mean the most to him. He kept a list of things that he wouldn't mind having,
but he had everything he wanted now. His partner had all the characteristics
listed in his journal, and their relationship was more fun and fulfilling than
he thought possible. Leif lived a happy and abundant life and his life
continued to get better every day.*

= =

Revisit your purpose, how and when you will achieve your purpose, the
schedule you will live by, the list of desires you have, and feel you have
everything already. Because you have your desires now, you no longer have
that feeling of lacking, wanting, or needing. Focus on the image and sensation
of your having your desires in this moment and visualize it in your mind, but

feel it with all your senses. Think of how it looks, feels, sounds, smells, and tastes.

Show yourself and the Universe you are following the plan to achieve your purpose and to receive everything you desire by initialing the following.

I promise I have:

_____   Defined my purpose.

_____   Stated what service, product or profession I provide in exchange for my fortune.

_____   Set a date for my success.

_____   Faith and confidence that I have everything I desire.

_____   Created my ideal schedule and live it now as closely as possible until I'm living it 100%.

_____   Visualized what I desire most with all 5 senses until imagination and reality are the same.

_____   Planned my best tomorrow before I go to sleep and first thing when I wake.

_____   Welcomed and embraced negative thoughts as they arise, without focusing on them, then replaced them with positive thoughts and feelings, knowing they do not define me, my purpose, or my life.

_____   Let go of any feelings of wanting or needing because I can see, feel, touch, taste, and smell what I have at this moment.

_____   Acted on all inspired ideas and thoughts as they come to me, and accepted them as guiding me on the path to achieving my purpose.

_____   Paid my bills by visualizing them as donations to my favorite people, businesses, charities, causes, events, and organizations.

_____ Kept a positive mindset, stayed focused on my purpose, and showed my appreciation and gratitude for everything in my life.

_____ Placed my order with the Universe for everything I want, and received them with the joy they give me now.

_____ Listed the characteristics of my ideal partner, imagined our life together, and made room in my life to receive them.

_____ Lived my true purpose to the best of my ability every day, knowing I create my own universe as I go along from here on out.

_____ Continued to read, watch, and listen only to inspirational media to help me stay positive and focused on achieving my purpose and everything I desire.

Remember the Key to the Secret from the steps in this workbook, and you'll be unstoppable in creating the life you want to live.

Chapter 16

Daily Affirmations

I am enough.

Thank you, thank you, thank you.

I am happy.

I am healthy.

I allow my body to heal itself.

Thank you for my perfect health and well-being.

I'm an excellent _____.

I'm a successful _____.

I'm a wealthy _____.

Everything good is coming to me today.

Magic and miracles follow me everywhere I go.

Everything happens as it should.

I am positive and joyful.

I appreciate everything I have.

I am confident.

I am powerful.

No just means, "Next!"

I am competent.

Breathe in..breathe out.

I am calm and connected.

I am loved.

I am taken care of.

I have faith.

I'm alive.

I have meaning.

I have purpose.

Tomorrow is a new day to begin.

I am open and receptive to wealth and abundance.

It's easy to manifest large sums of money.

The more money I have, the more I can give away.

I choose love and kindness.

When I change, my world changes with me.

I choose happiness.

I am aware.

Chapter 17

Inspirational Quotes

"A goal is a dream with a deadline." ~ Napoleon Hill

"The fundamental key to success is what you believe is true for yourself."
~ Oprah Winfrey

"It is a universal principle that you get more of what you think about, talk
about, and feel strongly about." ~ Jack Canfield

"Miracles come in moments. Be ready and willing." ~ Wayne Dyer

"He is a wise man who does not grieve for the things which he has not, but
rejoices for those which he has." ~ Epictetus

"It's a funny thing about life, once you begin to take note of the things you
are grateful for, you begin to lose sight of the things that you lack."
~ Germany Kent

"There is no scarcity of opportunity to make a living at what you love;
there's only scarcity of resolve to make it happen."
~ Wayne Dyer

"There is a truth deep down inside of you that has been waiting for you to
discover it, and that truth is this: you deserve all good things life has to
offer." ~ Rhonda Byrne

"I do what I love and I love what I do." ~ Unknown

"Abundance is not something we acquire. It is something we tune into."
~ Wayne Dyer

"I know I'm working in the right place with all the right people and that I learn all the valuable lessons my soul needs to learn."
~ Unknown

"The only limits in our life are those we impose on ourselves."
~ Bob Proctor

"I do what I do because of the passion that I feel." ~ Wayne Dyer

"Any idea, plan, or purpose may be placed in the mind through repetition of thought." ~ Napoleon Hill

"When we focus on our gratitude, the tide of disappointment goes out and the tide of love rushes in." ~ Kristin Armstrong

"Thoughts become things. If you see it in your mind, you will hold it in your hand." ~ Bob Proctor

"If the only prayer you said was thank you, that would be enough."
~ Meister Eckhart

"Everything you've ever wanted is sitting on the other side of fear."
~ George Addair

"As we express our gratitude, we must never forget that the highest appreciation is not to utter words, but to live by them."
~ John F. Kennedy

"You carry the passport to your own happiness."
~ Diane von Furstenberg

"The thought manifests as the word. The word manifests as the deed. The deed develops into habit. And the habit hardens into character. So watch the thought and its ways with care. And let it spring from love, born out of concern for all beings." ~ Buddha

About the Author

Dearest Reader,

This workbook is for you and about you. It is intended to help you fulfill your purpose by guiding you step-by-step on your journey to manifesting the life of your dreams faster than you thought possible.

I've been practicing the Law of Attraction since childhood, without knowing it. I started by finding the first star in the sky and reciting a popular nursery rhyme:

Star Light, Star Bright,
First star I see tonight,
Wish I may, wish I might,
Have the wish I wish tonight.

Then I would make my wish with all my heart. As a child, I forgot about my wish during the day, not realizing at the time it was the "letting go" part of the process.

When I became an adult, I stopped making wishes and reciting the poem, but I continued to receive what I set my mind to. After all, I had learned that wishes come true.

I wrote The Key to the Secret to share the epiphanies (inspired thoughts) that helped me connect the dots between the Law of Attraction teachings, religion, personal beliefs - whatever you want to call the inner voice that speaks to you. I hope learning to live presently, finding that satisfaction and bliss helps you be open to receiving everything you desire and that is intended for you.

Go through every step of the process. Feel it and live is now as closely as you can. When you can't physically do so, use your vibrant imagination to fool yourself into living it.

Remember The Key to the Secret and you'll be absolutely unstoppable.

~ Mina

~~~ Coming Soon! ~~~

The Key to the Secret Lock

Made in the USA
Columbia, SC
24 August 2024

41126789R00031